I'M SORRY
I HAVEN'T
A CLUE

With thanks to...

Toby Rushton, Tom Garden, Emma Darrell, Jill Foster, Jonathan James-Moore, Trevor Dolby, Iain Pattinson, Paul Merton, Stephen Fry, Tony Hawks, Jeremy Hardy, Bill Tidy, Denise Coffey, Kenny Everett, Mike Harding, Colin Sell, David and Shirley Scott, Samantha and Sven.

For Willie Rushton, 1937–1996.
Who left us all wanting more.

There was an old bugger called Rushton,
Who I will not salute in a hushed tone.
Wherever I look,
He's here in this book
With drawings and lines - how we miss him.

See how the rhymes suffer when he's not here?
Cheers, Will.
Baz.

I'M SORRY I HAVEN'T A CLUE

A CLUE

THE OFFICIAL LIMERICK COLLECTION

Tim Brooke-Taylor, Graeme Garden,
Barry Cryer, Willie Rushton,
Introduced by Humphrey Lyttelton

Compiled by Jon Naismith

ORION

First Published in 1998 by
Orion Media
an imprint of Orion Books Ltd
Orion House
5 Upper St Martin's Lane, London WC2H 9EA

By arrangement with the BBC
Based on the BBC Radio Programme
Jacket photograph courtesy of BBC Worldwide

A CIP catalogue record for this book is available
from the British Library

ISBN 0752817752

Printed and bound in Great Britain by
Butler & Tanner Ltd,
Frome and London

Contents

Introduced by Humphrey Lyttelton

I SUPPOSE YOU THINK you know all there is to know about limericks. That turns out on investigation to be precious little - and negative at that. For starters, the title has nothing to do with the Irish town of Limerick. True, word has been put about in the past that it derives from the chorus 'Will you come up to Limerick?' sung between impromptu and naughty verses composed at convivial parties. But to date, no one has ever been found to admit to singing such verses. Would you? Well then...

Even more far-fetched is the theory that the ribald verse-form was brought back to Limerick by veterans of the Irish Brigade in 1791 who had served in France for a hundred years. The evidence?

'Digerie, Digerie, Doge
La souris ascend l'horloge...'

Stop right there! Translated into English (presumably to avoid having to find a rhyme for 'horloge') that's 'Hickery, Dickery, Dock' - and any child of five knows that's not a limerick. It's not nearly filthy enough. As the writer E.V. Knox remarked rather sourly in his contribution on the sub-ject to the *Encyclopaedia Brittanica*, the example permits the verse-form 'almost as wide a licence in metre as it has latterly attained in morals.' All right, be like that.

Some people think that Edward Lear invented the limerick for his *Book of Nonsense* in 1846. (Make the most of this scholarship - it's all you're going to get.) Wrong again! He wasn't even very good at it, running out of steam - and rhyme - by line five and going back rather feebly to the beginning. To be fair, this did produce one masterpiece of anticlimax -

'There was an old person of Anerly
Whose conduct was strange and unmannerly:
He rushed down the Strand
With a pig in each hand,
But returned in the evening to Anerly.'

I dread to think what kind of punchline the teams of *I'm Sorry I Haven't A Clue* would have substituted for that. It has to be explained that, in the programme, they are fed an opening line by me and invent the rest taking a line at a time. The results, I venture to say, represent the apotheosis of the limerick, managing to be at once spontaneous, satirical, slick, scandalous, subversive and surrealistic.

Incidentally, I'm known to have had some success with words that begin with an 's'; I can reel off a list - though not when I m pissed - and will do so in moments of stress. I thought I'd just slip that in. Surreptitiously, of course.

Now where was I? Ah, yes - limericks. I could go on talking about them for another two sentences, but I must go. Have fun!

Humphrey Lyttelton

Unfortunate Openings

———

A cheeky young cow-poke called Hank,
Went into the woods with a plank.
For three or four winters,
He suffered the splinters,
But he laughed all the way to the bank.

There was a young lady called Chuck
(And we're all wishing Barry good luck)
'Twas an old merchant banker
Who finally sank her
With a highly-trained Muscovy duck.

They hailed her as Vivat Regina!
One night on an old ocean liner
A jolly jack tar
Went one step too far,
And it's a hell of a long way to China.

Bookworms

There's a lady who reads Mills and Boon
By the light of the silvery moon.
She loves all the stories,
And votes for the Tories,
They'll be coming to get her quite soon.

The best way to read Conan Doyle
Is sitting astride Katie Boyle.
When she cries: "PTO!"
That's the moment to go,
There are some things from which I recoil.

While pretending to read some Voltaire,
Strange noises emerged from my chair.
Then George Bernard Shaw
Said: "I'll open the door."
Thank God for a breath of fresh air!

While tucked up in bed with a Proust,
I was suddenly violently goosed,
And when I turned round,
To my horror I found
Barbara Cartland with corsets unloosed.

The Opposite S*x

A woman once said: "What the heck" to me,
"You look like a physical wreck to me;
You're a leery old gent
Still, come to my tent
Though it doesn't look very erect to me."

My wife and I sadly are parting,
In our lounge is a farm she is starting.
She's fed all the pigs
On syrup of figs,
No wonder my eyes are still smarting.

Saw this girl at the Henley Regatta,
Enjoying champagne and a natter.
I said: "Pardon me
Aren't you Rusty Lee?"
She said: "No, I am Jomo Kenyatta."

I'm suing my wife for divorce,
Since she had an affair with a horse.
I walked in one day,
There's this dappled grey –
He was chatting her up – what a sauce!

A Novel Approach

At a party with author Charles Dickens,
Lana Turner, Lord Reith and Slim Pickens.
Slim sat pickin' his nose,
Lord Reith doffed his clothes,
And Lana did tricks with some chickens.

The prime of Ms. Muriel Spark
Was in Brighton one night in the dark.
She met Graham Greene,
They did something obscene,
And next year they're going to Sark.

When you curl up in bed with a Trollope,
Fish and chips, mushy peas and a scallop,
With a nice cup of tea,
And the news on TV,
That's a wild night in old Nether Wallop.

"Having children," said Evelyn Waugh,
"Is really a bit of a bore.
We wanted a few
But when Auberon was two
We said: 'Oh let's not have any more.'"

Couch Potato

Last night I was watching *Blind Date*
When they brought on a chimp in a crate.
Cilla asked: "Who's for you?"
And the chimp said: "You'll do!"
And immediately started to mate.

One evening on *Crimewatch UK*
My heart was quite stolen away,
When Nick Ross confessed
That he'd pinched Sue Cook's vest,
And was exiled to Botany Bay.

Last week, if you saw *Panorama*,
It's clear that Ken Clarke is a charmer.
He's fat and he smokes,
And tells terrible jokes,
Like the one about Huntley and Palmer.

If you find you enjoy *Pebble Mill*
Then you're probably mentally ill.
Judy Spiers is no slouch
When it comes to the couch,
So lie back and keep perfectly still.

Steaming Brew

When drinking a cup of Earl Grey,
My trousers began to decay.
I clutched at my zip,
But the old PG tip
Was determined to have its own way.

Admirers of Lapsang Suchong
Always bang on a very large gong;
Like J. Arthur Rank,
Who we'd all like to thank
For kindly not coming along.

Consuming too much herbal tea
Can cause havoc when having a pee.
When out on the razzle
You tend to pass basil,
And last night old Basil passed me.

When sipping a cup of Darjeeling,
I observed that the brew was congealing.
It set like meringue,
Then went off with a bang!
And I found myself stuck to the ceiling.

19

Don't Get Your Vicars in a Twist

If you meet the Archbishop of York,
For God's sake don't offer him pork.
Well it is sort of true-ish,
He's just a bit Jewish.
Rabbi Blue told me – he's one to talk.

An old bishop – late of Bath and Wells –
Used to break up his room in hotels,
Then he'd rip off his gaiters,
Abuse several waiters,
Well he never was one for the gels.

A radical curate from Brent,
Who gave up entirely for Lent,
Just lay in the aisle
With a faraway smile,
And dreamt of the Duchess of Kent.

In the shower I bumped into the Pope.
He said: "I have given up hope."
Then he lay in the aisle
With a faraway smile,
While we hit him with soap-on-a-rope .

A Mixed Bouquet

While seated one day at the bidet,
My thoughts drifted right back to D-Day.
On Omaha beach
I enquired of this peach:
"How about it?" She said: "Quelle bonne idée".

The trouble with smoking in bed,
Is you find you set fire to your head
You go bald as a coot
And you're covered with soot.
"You're a prat," the fire officer said.

The stripper's pet Boa Constrictor
Would purr like a cat as he licked her.
He once bit her fan,
Poor innocent man
In the back of an old Vauxhall Victor.

"I like to dress up in a frock,"
Captain Kirk whispered fondly to Spock.
But when beamed up by Scottie
He emerged minus bottie,
And never got over the shock.

Tom Garden (13¾)

Sports Reports

In my car with the great Murray Walker,
He suddenly let loose a corker.
'Twas the first of a batch
In the pits at Brands Hatch.
He did the same thing in Majorca.

A strange fact about Tony Gubba
Is his fondness for eating whale blubber.
He starts off quite slow,
And then let's one go,
And folk say: "Can I smell burning rubber?"

Whenever I see Trevor Brooking,
He let's fly when nobody's looking.
He's very discreet,
It starts at his feet,
You can tell he likes Indian cooking.

When the studio guest's Jimmy Hill,
The aroma can make you feel ill.
While stroking his chin
He just can't keep it in:
The score's Arsenal: PHTHRRRP!!! Chelsea: nil.

Round Britain

I once spent a weekend in Hove
With a most unattractive old cove.
He said proudly: "I am
The great Jean Claude van Damme!"
But he wasn't - his Y-Fronts were mauve.

I once spent a weekend in Brighton
With the legendary Miss Enid Blyton.
She said: "You be Noddy
And I'll show you my body,"
But Big Ears kept turning the light on.

There is a young fellow from Ongar
Whose main joy in life is the Conga.
He's been dancing to date
Since 1908,
I don't *think* he'll be doing it much longer.

There was a young lady from Penge
Who had a day out with some friends.
She was given some fluid
By a randy old druid,
And now she's the toast of Stonehenge.

A Festive Garland

When out in the woods after holly
I heard someone shout: "Hello Dolly!"
It was Danny La Rue
Who said "How do you do?"
So I showed him, with the aid of my brolly.

There was an old skinflint called Scrooge
Who anointed his nipples with rouge.
Said: "I feel a right Charley,
But you should see Marley!
He's chained to a sailor in Bruges."

While Santa was out in his sleigh
He said: "How I love Christmas Day!
All over the earth
We rejoice in His birth."
And the reindeer all shouted: "Oy veh!"

When Santa gets bored in his grotto
He doesn't play bingo or lotto.
He sits on a shelf,
And toys with an elf,
"Sod this for a lark!" is his motto.

I Feel Like a Good Tune

In the middle of singing a hymn,
I was jostled by old Francis Pym.
He tripped over a hassock,
Looked right up my cassock,
And exclaimed: "Goodness me, hello Tim!"

In the middle of singing a carol,
Geoffrey Howe cried: "Your turn in the barrel."
"That's a bit of a bummer,"
Said John Selwyn Gummer,
As Cecil whipped off his apparel.

In the middle of singing an anthem,
The archbishop lisped: "My you're 'anthem."
At which Norman Lamont
Toppled into the font,
(He was pushed by an old bitch from Grantham).

In the middle of singing a psalm,
Michael Heseltine turned on the charm.
He shook his wild locks
And removed both his socks,
Which set off the fire alarms.

Herbal Mixture

They do say when cooking with chives:
"Wait till the fire engine arrives."
They tend to explode,
Then you dump your load.
I'm speaking to you from St Ives!

I have an aversion to dill.
I've been given an anti-dill pill.
Taken three times a day,
In an unusual way,
It still gives me a bit of a thrill.

There's something about oregano
That prevents you from singing soprano.
To hit a top C,
Take this tip from me,
Wear a truss made of rusty Meccano.

EEEK

OREGA

It's said that if Prince Charles eats sage.
He boils it until it turns beige.
The sage he likes most
Is Laurens Van der Post,
Who he keeps in a very small cage.

From A to B

If you're hoping to travel by train,
Then you're totally out of your brain.
You'll be squashed in the rush,
The compartment's a crush,
And you're wedged next to Robbie Coltrane.

In London if travelling by car,
You're unlikely to get very far.
It's deeply unpleasant,
Ah – Mornington Crescent!
Now nobody knows where we are.

When travelling in Holland by bike,
Something happened that I didn't like.
I had a mishap
When I hit a Dutch cap
And my finger got stuck in a dyke.

When deciding to travel by plane
You'll find it a hell of a strain.
The leg-room's too small,
There's no room at all,
And you're wedged next to Robbie again!

Cambridge Blues

A porter from Gonville and Caius
Grew potatoes on both of his knees.
On the end of his nose
Grew a rare kind of rose,
But you'll never guess where he grew these!

While out with a couple of Blues
I didn't know which one to choose.
The one with the squint,
Or the one in the splint?
I had both, I've got nothing to lose.

While out on the Cam in a punt,
I saw Reverend Spooner in front.
He said: "What a day gay!"
And: "Anchors aweigh!"
And: "Make way for my podding sunt!"

If you're studying Natural Science
I suggest that you wear an appliance.
You strap it on thus,
Then hop on a bus,
And you'll find you get masses of clients.

Hook, Line and Thinker

That miserable bloke Friedrich Nietzche
Had one most extraordinary feature.
He used it to pester
A fat tart called Esther,
But it luckily didn't quite reach her.

In the pub with St Thomas Aquinas,
I was rapidly struck by his shyness.
When I said: "It's your shout"
He quickly ran out.
So that was a bit of a minus.

A habit of Rene Descartes'
Was to eat very large baked bean tarts.
He became quite a cult,
The melodious result
Is now number eight in the charts.

A little known fact about Plato:
He invented the concept of NATO,
The Swiss Army Knife,
The Inflatable Wife,
And the Trouserless Jacket Potato.

News at Sixes and Sevens

When travelling abroad with Kate Adie,
She told me her background was shady.
She said: "I'm the love child
"Of the late Oscar Wilde
And someone called Bosey O'Grady."

At the Commons with newsman John Cole,
I enquired if he sang Rock and Roll.
He muttered: "I wish",
Then he took out a fish
And explained: "I can only sing Sole".

Whenever I watch Anna Ford
I sometimes cry out: "Praise the Lord!"
Oh goodness, love hurts
When you're starching your shirts,
And your trousers go stiff as a board.

While out with Sir Alastair Burnett,
I shouted: "Stand back, I'm a vet!"
He's been attacked by the Greens,
I said: "Quick nurse, the screens!"
And deftly removed a courgette.

A Selection From the Cheese Board

A Welshman who ate some Caerphilly
Said: "I love Wales because it's so hilly.
The girls in the valley
Are ever so pally.
They shout: 'Show us your...' don't be so silly."

A Frenchman who ate too much Brie
Shrugged his shoulders and said: "C'est la vie!
That's enough of that stuff
'Cos an oeuf is an oeuf.
I shall 'ave one on toast for my tea."

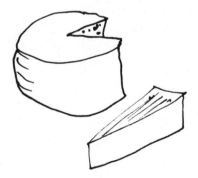

An Italian who loved parmesan
Broke wind in the back of his van.
With an ear-splitting roar
It blew off the door,
So it's arrividerci Milan.

A Greek who would only eat feta
Once crept up behind Henrietta.
He bowed very low
And shouted: "Hello!"
Then shoved his head right up her sweater.

Play That Thing

A man with a gift for the fiddle
Liked his steaks very rare on the griddle.
He played tunes multifarious
On his fine Stradivarius,
With "a present from Rhyl" through the middle.

While playing some scales on the flute,
I noticed strange stains on my suit.
Am I losing my bottle?
I'm covered in dottle!
Does James Galway get this in mid toot?

While learning to play the bassoon,
In a bordello in downtown Rangoon,
My reputation for blowing
Got all the girls going,
Oh these Burmese girls love a good tune.

At the sound of a lone clarinet,
I shouted: "Stand back, I'm a vet!"
Picture Acker's alarm
As I thrust in my arm.
Oh God, I still drink to forget!

Pathfinders

While exploring with Captain James Cook,
He gave me an old fashioned look.
He said: "Hello sailor!
Tell me, who's your tailor?
It must be that nice man Tim Brooke."

A habit of Vasco da Gama's
Was to tear off the first mate's pyjamas.
Then he'd wave them about
And give a great a shout:
"I wish you were here, Judith Chalmers!"

When out sailing with Sir Francis Drake
We discovered Veronica Lake.
We climbed Peggy Mount,
Jimmy Hill doesn't count,
Scaling Cliff was a dreadful mistake.

The odd thing about Cecil Rhodes
Was his fondness for natterjack toads.
He'd eat them alive,
Sometimes three, four or five,
Hence his need for enormous commodes.

Odds and Gods

In the woods once I thought I saw Pan,
A strange creature – half goat and half man.
His father was Billy
His mother was silly
They met on *Blind Date* in Japan.

That mythical creature the Sphinx
Is smarter than anyone thinks.
He sits there and smirks
And you don't think it works,
Then when you're not looking, it winks.

When out clubbing with Helen of Troy
She suggested this interesting ploy:
She said: "Make a big horse
Out of plywood, of course
And stick it together with gloy."

There's a rumour that Oedipus Rex
Had a terrible Mother Complex.
His poor mum Jocasta
Was a walking disaster,
But at least she took traveller's cheques.

The Great Detectives

That remarkable sleuth Hercule Poirot
Was attacked by an over-sexed moirrot.
He said: "I've got your number
You naughty cucumber!
I'll see you the same time tomoirow!"

"Here's a strange case!" said Watson to Holmes.
"Outside there are two garden gnomes.
One's lost his wee rod,
And the other poor sod
Has been sat on by Nicholas Soames!"

Did you hear about old Van der Valk?
He powders his bottom with talc.
When they asked him: "What for?"
He said: "My bum's red raw.
You can see by the way that I walk."

The thing about Inspector Morse
Is that now he is right back on course.
In Provence for a year
He's revived his career
As the back of a pantomime horse.

A Good Hand

While playing a tough game of patience
I was savaged by several alsatians.
In quite severe pain
I jumped on a train,
And continually flushed between stations.

At a party we all played strip poker.
I was sat between Cher and Bram Stoker,
When old Brian Clough
Stripped down to the buff,
It was then that Frank Bough played his joker.

One evening while playing at whist
My partner leaned forward and hissed:
"That's your tenth double gin
You've a vacuous grin
In a word – ah you're getting the gist."

While playing a game of bezique
I was jumped on by Zorba the Greek.
He grabbed my bazooki,
Cried: "How's this for nookie?"
And I couldn't sit down for a week.

One evening while playing Canasta
My hostess produced some warm pasta
Poured it over my head
And jovially said:
"How's that for an albino rasta?"

Tales from Chaucer

As I reached for my copy of Chaucer
I awkwardly fell on a saucer.
I started to swoon,
When I noticed the spoon...
At this point the story gets coarser.

In the pub with this old Wife of Bath,
She sat herself down by the hearth.
She lifted her skirt,
Said: "Don't think me a flirt,
It's a terribly well-trodden path."

I've met this unusual Monk
Dressed up as a pineapple chunk.
He lifts up his habit,
Invites you to grab it,
And then the wee tease does a bunk.

While out with a Doctor of Physick,
He slipped me a strong analgesic.
I fell to the ground,
When I woke up I found
I was chained to a lamp-post in Chiswick.

A Beauty of Bevvies

One lunchtime while quaffing some ale,
George Bush's heart started to fail.
And things got much worse
When a well-meaning nurse
Said: "Don't worry I've sent for Dan Quayle."

After tasting a bottle of wine,
The Pope shouted: "Your place or mine?"
I said: "I'll give you a call."
So he wrote on the wall
His phone number: VAT 69.

The medicinal power of brandy
Is vouchsafed, so keep some of it handy.
Its wondrous effect
Kept Churchill erect,
All the same, it did sod all for Ghandi.

After drinking large measures of port,
You may find that you've been caught short,
And you're miles from the Gents –
Well it seems to make sense –
Shove the cork up your arse – just a thought!

Bless This Scouse

I once had a trial with Bill Shankly –
At the end he just looked at me blankly.
Said: "You're no Roger Hunt,
In fact I'll be blunt,
You're absolute rubbish quite frankly."

I once had a blind date with Cilla,
I took her to watch Aston Villa.
She sang to the crowd,
And she sang very loud,
And that's why they threatened to kill her.

Last night at a show by Ken Dodd.
The usherette said: "Oh my God!
He'll go on for years,
He's bound to sing *Tears*
When he finishes, give us a prod."

Out drinking with Bruce Grobelaar,
He paid with some cash from a jar.
He said: "See, I saved this!"
So I gave him a kiss,
And he tipped himself over the bar.

Menagerie à Trois

I once had a date with a ferret
Thus earning the Order of Merit.
For dating a bee
I got the V.C.
Which my offspring will one day inherit.

I once had a Smart-Alec gerbil
Who did nothing but bumble and burble.
His one saving grace
Was to sit on my face
And impersonate Ivan the Terbil.

A horny young owl in the zoo
Fell in love with a gay caribou.
He slipped out one night
In search of delight
Saying: "D'you fancy an odd cockatoo?"

A lion with a surgical truss
Said: "I don't want to make any fuss
But that damn unicorn,
Keeps showing me soft porn,
It's not a thing that I care to discuss."

Man-Made Soul

In Tesco's with Earth, Wind and Fire,
Mr Wind assaulted a buyer.
Mr Fire then hit Earth,
Who promptly gave birth.
"Tesco's, News at Ten, Barry Cryer."

My hamster is called Otis Redding.
My goldfish is Joan Armatrading.
My dogs are the Platters –
Not that that matters –
We're all up to here with the wedding.

The artist formerly known as Prince,
On stage he would posture and mince.
Then just for a giggle
Changed his name to a squiggle,
And nobody's heard of him since.

When it snows you will find Sister Sledge
Out mooning at night on the ledge.
One storey down
Is the maestro James Brown,
Displaying his meat and two veg.

Fruit and Veg

While squeezing the juice from a lime
I found I was stuck for a rhyme.
My first thought was: "Orange",
And then I thought: "Pint",
Good God, is that really the time?

The best way to eat avocado
Is underneath Miss Brigitte Bardot.
Well it was in the forties,
When I practised my naughties,
With the help of old Dr Barnardo.

One Christmas I lost my satsuma.
No, not there! There's no truth in the rumour.
No, not under my hat,
Up my trousers, you prat!
My God, have you no sense of humour?

After eating a large bowl of prunes
I put on a tape of the Goons.
I suddenly laughed,
There's a fearful noise aft,
And bang go my blue pantaloons!

The Great Dictators

At the seaside I saw Mussolini
Struggle into a tight brown bikini.
I said: "Hold hard Benito,
This must spell finito
Now I've seen where you keep your Zuccini."

At lunch with Attila the Hun
I ordered a roast corn-fed nun.
He said: "We have monks
Served on pineapple chunks."
I said: "All right" and he gave me one.

A weakness of Vlad the Impaler
Was to shout out at men: "Hello sailor!"
In far Transylvania
He'd indulge his mania,
Dressed up as Elizabeth Taylor.

My anorak's Idi Amin's.
My corset was H.M. The Queen's.
My large wonderbra
Once belonged to the Shah,
And these are Roy Hattersley's jeans.

Channel Hopping

While tuned into BBC1,
I was lying in bed with a nun.
I decided to stop
When a flash-bulb went: "Pop!"
I'm now on page three of *The Sun*.

When turning on BBC2
I thought: "They need something brand new.
Something witty and funny,
Which doesn't cost money,
Why not '*Sorry I Haven't A Clue*'?"

If you regularly watch ITV,
(Which I gather is on Channel Three)
They've got jolly good breaks
With commercials for cakes,
It's the programmes that mystify me.

If you happen to watch Channel Four,
You must be a bit of a bore.
You can see Richard Whiteley
Not once, but twice nightly,
I don't think I can take any more.

Treading the Bards

That potty old monarch King Lear
Was a martyr to chronic diarrhoea.
He'd sit on his throne,
Emit a loud groan,
And nobody else would go near.

That warrior Coriolanus
Did several things that were heinous.
He tortured the cat,
Set fire to my hat,
And now he's been sick in my trainers.

That jealous old soldier Othello
Let out a stentorian bellow.
He fell on his sword,
And shouted: "Oh Gawd!
That's the last time that I'll play the cello."

At an orgy old Julius Caesar,
Met a virgin and tried hard to please her.
She said: "My name's Mimi,
Are you pleased to see me?
Or is that the tower of Pisa?"

It Can't Get Verse Than This

A romantic named Percy Bysshe Shelley
Said this of Liza Minelli:
"While one of her breasts
Is admired by my guests,
The other one looks like George Melly."

An exciting young poet named Keats
Was renowned for his dare-devil feats.
He'd dance and he'd sing,
Then belch 'God Save The King'.
He was very well paid for repeats.

At a seance with W. B. Yeats
He'd asked along several blind dates.
The table was rising,
It's hardly surprising,
He'd cracked open a packet of Mates.

"I'm depressed" said the Laureate Ted Hughes.
"Forty years on the throne, where's the muse?"
Then inspired, he wrote
Of a three legged stoat
Disembowelling dead kangaroos.

Can't Cook, Won't Eat

Dining alone with Keith Floyd
Is something we all should avoid.
Everything's fine
Till he gets to the wine,
And then he's a right haemorrhoid.

If you go in the kitchen with Delia,
Beware, for she's certain to feel ya.
She'll fondle your rump,
Then carve off a lump,
And the ointment takes ages to heal ya.

The technique of the two Brothers Roux
Is to throw everything in the stew.
They call it: "Pot Luck"
And you're instantly struck
By memories of Regent's Park Zoo.

"Pass the wok then," said Hudson to Halls.
"I'm sorry, I fear nature calls."
"Stop that you fat Kiwi!"
"It's only a wee wee!
It might even improve the Prawn Balls."

Creepy-Crawlies

I once had a fully trained moth
Who'd swim like a fish in Scotch Broth.
To end his routine
He'd fart 'God Save The Queen'.
Has anyone here got a cloth?

For a laugh I dressed up as a bee.
Blame Anthea Turner not me.
She was dressed as a rose,
But I'm not into those,
So I stung the poor cow on the knee.

As a child I was troubled by nits,
Which I caught when we stayed at the Ritz.
We moved to the Savoy,
Where a rogue saveloy
Leapt up and thrilled granny to bits.

I've a cockroach that sings like a thrush.
Its song fills the evening hush.
The sound of its screech
Thrills the parts you can't reach,
And that's quite an adrenalin rush!

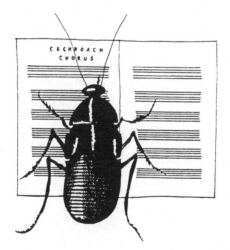

North of the Border

While out on the banks of Loch Ness
I was startled to see Rudolf Hess.
He shouted: "Who's won?"
The ignorant Hun,
I said: "You did, in the end, more or less."

The thing about wearing a kilt
Is it tends to reveal how I'm built.
But should you chance your arm,
It has an alarm,
And my sporran lights up and says: "Tilt!"

Last night I was roused by the pipes
Being played by a band of strange types.
They then tossed a caber,
And shouted: "Vote Labour!"
My sporran lit up and said: "Cripes!"

I've a small breed of dog called a Scottie,
Who's house-trained and sits on a potty.
He gives a loud yap,
The mischievous chap,
Then stands up and wipes his wee bottie.

Compose Yourself

I've an enormous collection of Strauss
The *Blue Danube* runs through my house.
Johann himself,
I have stuffed on a shelf
By my inflatable Sir Stanley Rous.

One evening while listening to Brahms,
The vicar's wife leapt in my arms.
In the ensuing mellee,
They danced on my belly
And set off the fire alarms.

A little-known fact about Lizst
That listeners may well have missed.
He played ludo and lotto,
While partially blotto
But he had to be pissed to play whist.

When Johann Sebastian Bach
Was asked what he did after dark,
He said: "I compose a Te Deum,
And perhaps a Requiem
Then I pop out and flash in the park."

Strut Your Funky Stuff

The art of the old highland reel
Is to spin round upon your left heel.
Then you waggle your dirk,
With a bit of a smirk;
At least those are my grounds for appeal.

At a party when doing the rumba,
Down my trousers I thrust a cucumber.
"My God, what is that?"
Cried a girl in a hat,
So I gave her my telephone number.

When invited to a Morris Dance
I strap on my bells in advance.
"My God, what is that?"
Cried a girl in a hat,
"Another cucumber perchance?"

For those who enjoy a gavotte,
I do, I admit it, a lot.
Hundreds of nights
Leaping round in my tights,
And it does keep the vegetables hot.

The Pleasures of the Orient

There's a lady I knew in Calcutta,
Who spoke with a very slight stutter.
Her impediment
Was delightful, it lent
Such charm when she'd utter "B-butter".

The pleasures of old Singapore
Are seductive - you cry out for more.
There's massages and rubs
And dubious clubs
With unspeakable things on the floor.

How well I remember Hong Kong,
It reminds me of that old sweet song
That I heard in a disco
About San Francisco
Hang on – I think I've got that wrong.

Don't forget, when you visit Bangkok
The ex-pats are a bit of a shock.
If they've no watch or clock,
On your door they will knock
And shout: "Got the time on ya cock?"

This Sporting Life

I only once dabbled in Croquet
(My psychiatrist gave me the OK)
I spent happy hours
Whacking balls into flowers
Which made an unusual bouquet.

At a championship final in Bowls,
The green was invaded by moles.
They dug up the drains,
Colonel Fawcett's remains
And some very old British Rail rolls.

One night when we played Table Tennis
Overlooking the Grand Canal, Venice,
Cried a stout gondolier:
"Look what I gotta here!"
It was Neil and his lovely wife Glenys.

While out for a game of Badminton
I asked the young Pro for a hint on
Care of my shuttlecock.
He said: "One – an old sock
Or two – fewer weekends in Frinton."

Indoor Games

One evening while playing mah jong
I suddenly burst into song.
My song was inspired
By some lads from a Triad
Doing unmentionable things with a prong.

One evening at Trivial Pursuit
I got: "Who played the name role in Klute?"
Without pausing to ponder
I called out: "Jane Fonda!"
But it wasn't of course it was Donald Sutherland.

The Gossiping Ghoul

There was a young girl called Bianca
Who said as she sipped Ferni Branca:
"I'm thoroughly sick
So I'm leaving you Mick,"
And he didn't know quite how to thank her.

I take off my hat to Frank Bough.
It's terribly easy to scoff,
But that man is a whizz,
He certainly is!
Ain't he great! Ain't he grand! Switch him off!

A bouncy page three girl called Sam
Said: "For clothing I give not a damn!"
To be totally bare
She shaved off her hair,
And now she's the King of Siam.

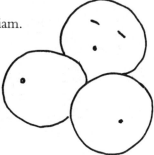

Eating Out

Last night I had curry for dinner
At the Taj Mahal Palace, in Pinner.
I cried: "Waiter! Hey you!
There's a mess in the loo!"
He replied: "No sir, that's Michael Winner."

One evening while eating Chinese,
I spilt sweet and sour on my knees.
My trousers exploded,
My socks were corroded,
I went home in a pair of lychees.

One evening while eating jugged hare,
I suddenly spied Lionel Blair.
He stood on one leg,
And ate a boiled egg,
Which showed quite exceptional flair.

One evening while eating tandoori
I was seized by a raven-haired houri.
I gave such a start,
My zip burst apart –
At least that's my defence to the jury.

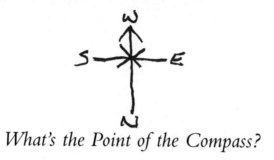

What's the Point of the Compass?

I was courting a girl from the North
Who in the sack-race had come fourth.
She had a slight lisp
But her diction was crisp
When she said: "Get your hand out my drawth!"

I was courting a girl from the South
Who had a most kissable mouth.
But my friend from the North
Said: "You realithe of courth
She'th built like the thide of a howth."

I was courting a girl from the East
Who was Ipswich's first woman priest.
She was tall, blond and lissom
And loved exorcism
Dial 666 and ask for the beast.

I was courting a girl from the West
Who had a tattoo on her chest.
'Twas a portrait of Gazza
And each one who has her
Says: "Blimey love, pull down your vest!"

Living legends

At an orgy with Sir Jimmy Savile
His track suit began to unravel
He said: "Don't make a fuss,"
And fashioned a truss
From cement – two parts sand, three parts gravel.

While having a drink with Ken Bruce
I noticed his trousers were loose
I said: "You need a belt
You unspeakable Celt."
He said: "I've just had twelve on the hoose."

At afternoon tea with John Peel
I enquired if his accent was real.
He said: "Out of the house
I'm incredibly Scouse,
But at home it depends how I feel."

At a restaurant with veteran Pete Murray
He demolished a vindaloo curry.
There came a great roar
That rattled the floor,
And laid waste vast areas of Surrey.

Read All About It!

On thumbing my way through *The Sun*
On page three was an old topless nun
Since Murdoch found God
His behaviour's quite odd
But as he says: "It's all good clean fun."

While reading the *Exchange & Mart*
A terrible noise made me start.
But I didn't worry
It was only Pete Murray
And with him it's not rude it's an art.

While leafing my way through *The Times*,
I read the bizarrest of crimes.
It appears in Rangoon
A man sued a baboon.
Not funny, but be fair it rhymes.

I saw in this morning's *Express*
Prince Charles in a transparent dress.
Oh – is that the Royal Show?
The Queen shouted: "No!"
But the man from Del Monte said: "Yes!"

New Balls Please

That extraordinary grunting from Seles
Her opponents describe as quite hellish.
The noise she is making
You'd swear she was faking
But it's something the gentlemen relish.

While serving to Billie Jean King
I suddenly heard a loud "ping!"
To roars of applause,
She slipped on new drawers
Which the umpire'd remembered to bring.

There's a rumour about Yannick Noah:
In the showers he's a bit of a goer.
He pretends he's an owl,
With the aid of a towel,
Two balls and a pink feather boa.

On a court with the Swede Mats Wilander,
I couldn't help taking a gander.
His shorts were so tight,
Oh I say, what a sight!
No wonder his grip's a two-hander.

Foreign Climes

While washing my smalls in Bangkok –
Where you bash them quite hard on a rock –
By the banks of a creek,
I let out a shriek
When I missed them and mangled my sock.

There was a young girl from Sri Lanka,
Who had an affair with a banker.
She gave him her all,
He made a withdrawal,
And didn't even bother to thank her.

A Portuguese goer from Chile,
Once met a young hooker called Willie.
He started to hug her,
She said: "Let's play rugger."
Half time score: Chile-Three, Willie-Nillie.

A belly dancer hot from Jakarta,
Went back to her old Alma Mater.
She kept the school waiting,
To see her gyrating
'Til somebody pressed her self-starter.

A Night at the Opera

I've never been one for Peer Gynt,
The mere mention, my face turns to flint.
The reasons are legion,
Number one – he's Norwegian,
Number two – he pissed off with my bint.

If like me you can't stand La Bohème
(I was right, I can hear bubbling phlegm)
Then you'll doubtless concur
There's something odd about her.
Still, I've heard Figaro's one of them.

There are people addicted to Tosca
Well there's Nigel and Clifford and Oscar
And a cheerful old sport
Who sent in this report
"John Cole, Bay Bay Seer, Moddogoscar".

The first time I saw Wagner's Ring
How I prayed the fat lady would sing.
That would mean it was over,
I could go home to Rover
Oh the Ring is a terrible thing.

Round Britain Again

There's a cafe in old Milton Keynes,
Where the waiter wears very tight jeans,
With an awfully large bulge
Which when asked he'll divulge
Is in fact seven tins of baked beans.

A warped taxidermist from Stoke,
Was stuffing a pig in a poke.
Said the porker: "Hey Fred!
I'm very far from dead,
Is this your idea of a joke?"

At a party near Jodrell Bank
I've forgotten how much we all drank.
The snag with an orgy,
As I said to Boy Georgie,
Is when you leave you don't know who to thank.

I once spent a weekend in Rhyl
I'd gone there in search of a thrill
We passed through
Llanfairpwllgwyngyllgogerychwyrndrobwyllllanty-
siliogogogoch,
Which gave me a shock,
I thought Llanfairpwllgwyngyllgogerychwyrndrobwyll-
llantysiliogogogoch was in Brazil.

Songsters

There is a young lad called Rod Stewart
Just give him a song and he'll screw it.
He sings through his sporran,
Pulls anything foreign,
A damn good trick if you can do it.

Barry Manilow's rather a freak,
Some say that he's well past his peak.
On one of his shows
He unblocked his nose,
I heard it on *Pick Of The Week*.

Michael Jackson's a bit of a card
Every bit of himself he'll discard.
He's rebuilt his face
From all over the place,
So his buttocks are terribly scarred.

Have I Got Shoes For You

I once found my pet puss in Boots,
Buying condoms and herbal cheroots.
I said: "Naughty cat,
You mustn't do that
They'll think we're a couple of fruits."

Whenever I wear my new clogs,
I'm followed by frisky young dogs.
One started to beg,
Then cocked his leg
And dampened the hem of my togs.

Whenever I wear winklepickers,
The footsteps behind are the vicar's.
It's the backs of my shoes
He likes to peruse –
Or perhaps it's the cut of my knickers.

You won't guess what I keep in my wellies:
Three tarts and a couple of jellies,
A Cadbury's Flake
And a portion of hake
And an old spotted dick of George Melly's.

Holy Ridiculous

A bishop and I shared a gherkin
As we knocked back the ale by the firkin.
He said: "During confessions
I do farmyard impressions:
Cluck! cluck! cluck! Well it's better than working."

 "Posing naked can often be fun,"
Said the priest with a wink to the nun.
She replied: "But I'm chaste,"
He said: "Oh what a waste,
I've seen worse on page three of *The Sun*."

Hooray for the Venerable Bede
Who frequently scattered his seed.
Twixt alter and pew,
He would seek postures new,
And whenever it rained, cry: "God's peed."

A Fragrant Nosegay

A train driver told his young stoker:
"It's time for a game of strip poker.
It's a grand thing to do
As you're speeding through Crewe,
And when Elsie gets on we'll de-coke her."

Whilst probing my nose with a poker
To the strains of the old Kari-oka,
I lit up a fag
Who hit me with his bag
Crying: "Excuse me, this is a non smoker!"

As she swallowed her fifth jellied eel,
She cried: "Ooh I just love how they feel!"
But the sixth eel was limp,
So she gobbled a shrimp,
Now she stars in prawn movies in Deal.

An alternative Coco the Clown
Pulled his trousers up rather than down.
His nose was bright green,
And mildly obscene;
You should see where he painted his frown.

I'm Sorry I Haven't a Clue

———————

I'm sorry I haven't a clue
So tell me just what would you do.
We haven't much time
So answer in mime...
Oh I see, very well, same to you.

A brilliant young chairman called Humph,
Who was always surrounded by bumph,
Kicked his legs in the air
Ran a comb through his hair –
For him an extraordinary triumph.

The teams are renowned for their wit,
They're convinced that the show is a hit.
They say; "Week after week
We hit a new peak!"
But the audience knows that it's rubbish.

There is an old man of Hatch End,
Old watches and clocks he will mend.
He paints them bright red
Then he takes them to bed;
It's driving his wife round the bend.

When they raised the Titanic they found
That the band had survived and not drowned.
They hadn't gone far,
They were still at the bar,
And that is why Humph's still around.